T0147141

A Voice Will Run

JOHN F CARVER

authorHOUSE®

AuthorHouse™
1663 Liberty Drive
Bloomington, IN 47403
www.authorhouse.com
Phone: 833-262-8899

Published by AuthorHouse 10/21/2022

ISBN: 978-1-6655-7265-1 (sc)
ISBN: 978-1-6655-7266-8 (hc)
ISBN: 978-1-6655-7267-5 (e)

Library of Congress Control Number: 2022918442

Print information available on the last page.

Dedicated to my mother who was a good listener.

Contents

The Voice of Family

The Voice of Work

The Voice of Love

The Voice of Time

The Voice of Faith

The Voice of Desert Places

The Voice of Meditation

Short Stories

A Special Place

Down by the land where the Eldeberry grows,
Near the banks of the swift Allegheny,
We laid down our weapons of war,
And took up the tools of peace.

Hammer and saw, shovel and pick,
Hard we worked in the rich green valley,
Cutting and clearing, building and shaping.
We played in the forest,
And looked for lichens on its soft damp ground.

It was ours and there was nothing like it we thought.
It was like a secret place.
But we wanted to share it with those we knew;
If only they would come and see.

6/93

The Voice of Sacrifice

Watch

They came, the people,
To the tomb,
The tomb of the unknown,
The Tomb of the Unknown Soldier.
In silence they watched
As the soldier without rank,
Marched in solemn cadence
To guard the remains,
Of the soldier of unknown rank
Who had made the ultimate sacrifice.

At the changing of the guard
An aged veteran came, hobbled and out of breath,
Worn from time and the wounds of war.
Blocked by the crowd, he could not see
To pay respect to his fallen comrade.
Hearing him they turned and,
Like a sea of people they parted,
And let him pass to the front of the silent crowd,
Close to the fallen soldier.

Then they resumed their watch
At the tomb,
The tomb of the unknown,
The Tomb of the Unknown Soldier.

June, 2004

Honor

They of the Eagle, Globe, and Anchor found,
A fallen comrade on the ground.
Reverently they took him up,
And brought him to the waiting truck.
They draped me across his body length,
Symbol of our life and strength.
White stars and blue about his head,
Then stripes of purity, stripes blood red.

At Iwo Jima they raised me high,
My spirit prevailed, though many died.
They carried me at Belleau Wood,
Where Marine battalions firmly stood.
I led them through the gas and fog,
As Germans cried out, "DEVIL DOGS!"
But no greater honor have I done,
Than to be the shroud for this brave son.

4/27/03

Longing

On reading Bradley's "Flags of our Fathers."

When the sun goes down,
And the moon goes up,
And all is quiet and still,
The ghosts of Iwo's battle past,
Rise up, upon the hill.

They peer across the vast deep blue,
And strain to see their land,
Where children play and couples stroll
Walking hand in hand.

Their faces light with smiles of joy,
To know that freemen reign.
With all the carnage and the cost,
Their deaths were not in vain.

Their courage and commitment,
Had won a worthy cause.
Their people live and prosper
Within the land of laws.

Somberly, in deep despair they wish,
A ship could take them home,

To anxious loved ones' outstretched arms
Beneath the heavens' dome.

Then back into their graves they lay,
To rest another day,
Knowing that their sacrifice
Was freedom's price to pay.

8/30/2006

Anthem of Honor

I went to the shores of Hawaii,
The gem of the peaceful sea.
Its stately peaks and balmy breeze
Were everything to me.

On one of those lush green islands,
Is a harbor they call Pearl.
No finer place to shelter ships
Is found in all the world.

The Japanese attacked there,
With bursting bombs and lead.
They smote our fleet asunder,
And left us all for dead.

But my father and many like him,
Rose up to heed the call.
He went to war at seventeen,
And faced the acrid pall.

He rode the North Atlantic,
And took the secret code.
And fed the red-hot eight-inch guns,
Then prayed, and sent the load.

The war they fought is won now,
And freedom's flag still flies.
The veterans all are aging fast,
And share their storied lives.

So I see the Arizona,
With its dirge of watery graves,
And I miss my father's presence
To salute the young and brave.

To tell them, "We went on boys!"
In silent prayer's embrace.
"Your lives live on, in victory,
In strength, in truth, in grace."

10/21/02

Waiting

They waited.
The Great Aunts,
By the campfire,
Deep in the heart of the Alleghenies,
With their nieces and nephews,
And children's children,
As they waited so many times before,
Through World War II, Korea,
Vietnam, The Gulf War.
They waited far into the night,
Weary and watchful.

They were waiting for the Marine,
Who had come out of the deserts of Iraq,
Into the Persian Gulf and the Arabian Sea,
Through the Suez and into the blue Mediterranean,
Headed west, always west,
Across the waves of the cold Atlantic,
To the shores of Lejeune.
Then through the great state of North Carolina,
And over the winding mountain roads of West Virginia,
To the enchanted Alleghenies.

Up the steep concrete road he came, honking his horn.
When he got out of his car into the pitch dark,

His mother came to embrace him,
A long embrace filled with emotion.
Then he walked into the firelight,
Tall and slender, haircut "high and tight"
Deeply darkened by the sun.
He embraced the aunts,
And they welcomed him,
Happy their prayers had been answered,
Happy to see him back safely home.
Then feeling the flesh of warm,
And knowing that body and soul were still united,
They retired to their cabins to rest for another day.

11/24/03

The American Soldier

There was no crown where I was born,
The land was new and free.
I laid my life down on the ground
In love of liberty.

In Pacific jungles filled with hate,
And bayonets affixed,
I fought at Shiloh's Hornets Nest,
And crossed the river Styx.

In bloody revolution
I marched in freezing cold.
With meager rags for combat boots,
My feet turned red the snow.

In home, and mill, and office,
Remember if you can,
With determined, bold defiance,
I upheld the rights of man.

Circa March 2008

The Voice of a Place

Allegheny Reflection

My Grandfather's cabin lies in its niche
In the great mountains of the Alleghenies.
I must go there.
The stillness will sooth my heart
As a small child's feet soothe a tired father's back
As they walk across it.
My Grandfather built the first cabin with his bare hands;
But man's civilization needed a reservoir.
So, the valley my grandfather's cabin lay in was flooded.
He moved up the hill above the manmade roadway.
He still goes there; as often as possible.
He has a trailer now.
His bones are stiff and he has grown old,
And he can't do the big strong things
He used to do when I watched him as a young boy.
But he still goes there. It is his place.
To be alone – and to work, and cultivate,
As one does a rose which one loves so much.

Spring 1973

I Remember the Place

I remember the place we had down below.
Near the edge of the road, the pine tree so tall,
The clear mountain air and the Whip-o-will's call;
And all of us gathered 'round the campfire's glow.
Returning from war with a new life to sow,
We worked through the day until almost nightfall.
Digging deep for the piers and putting up walls.
Then fixing the roof with the hammer's sharp blow.

And giving our all in our work and our play
The great logs we would split with wet sinews strong,
Then hike through the woods till the end of the day.
When the deep winter snows brought the nights so long
Our sleek sleds cut a path down the trail's curved way.
Then again, in the spring, the Robin's sweet song.

November 2001

The Well

When my grandfather sat down
After some long strenuous task
He said, "Johnny get me a drink
Of water from the well."
I ran into the house, fetched a glass
And then went to the pump.
I pumped and pumped.
The water flowed out
Gushing down the wooden trough
Onto the gravelly ground and into the earth.
My hand tested the water until it went numb.
Then I filled the glass until it spilled over
With clear, sparkling cold spring water.
Very carefully I walked to where
Grandpa sat under the shade tree
In front of the cabin.
He took the sweating glass
And held it for a moment,
Rejoicing in its ice-cold gift.
"Ahh Johnny that looks good," he said.
And with one long draught
He emptied the glass of its thirst quenching contents.

"Ahhh that was good," he said.
"You're a good 'Joe' Johnny."
I was happy he was so pleased.

Circa 1973

Song of the Allegheny

I will go away now.
Down to nowhere,
Up to "the mountains."
I will follow the road with the endless line.
Out of the city,
Past the farmlands of the Wasichu[1],
Past the land he has raped,
Past the land he has subdued,
Past the land he has consumed,
To the mountains of the Allegheny,
To a place nestled in the woods.

We dug a well there,
The water was sparkling pure.
It must have been God's well,
The water made pure and sweet
With the touch of his lips.
We built a Place there.
Something told my grandfather,
"If you build it, he will come"[2]
And Great Grandfather came,
A finished carpenter by trade,
(My brothers inherited his gift).

---

[1] Sioux word for whiteman.
[2] From movie "Field of Dreams".

He built our Place with the help of many hands.
One, two, three additions we made.
Like a longhouse for family.
Beams of young, solid oak were its strength.
From stuff the Wasichu did not want,
We built our Place.
Though made of old it was new in spirit.
It was made whole in us.

We shared everything there;
Our work, our food,
Our things, our thoughts,
On projects, at meals, at play,
By the fireplace at night.
It was as though we were one.
One with the oaks of the mountain.
One with the Whip-o-will of the treetops.
One with the fireflies at night.
One with each other,
One with our God.

Across the street of the endless line,
Was the Reservation.
We were told never to go there.
It belonged to the Indians.
We held it in great respect,
For it was all the Wasichu left him.
The Indians knew us to be peaceful,
And did not harm our Place.
My Uncle of the Dark Eyes knew many of them,
And lived with them in harmony man years before.

Often Grandfather and Grandmother
Would go for a walk at night.
He leading with a flashlight.

She walking by his side.
The light of the firefly,
And the chirp of the cricket
Were their companions.
On clear nights the sky was filled with stars.
So many we could not count them.
They walked together alone.
Sharing the day,
Or walking in silence.
At ease in each other's company.

Then the dam came.
The reservoir that drove us from our Place.
The Wasichu wanted to control the Allegheny.
He wanted to keep the water level always the same,
For the city by the three rivers,
Where the raging fire mills were.
They made the silvery gray metal there
That built their cities and stripped the earth
For their god called Progress.

Though the Wasichu took our Place,
I never saw my grandfather cry.
He might have alone, but I did not see him.
I think he did not cry because if he did,
He might not stop.
Instead, he gave up a part of his heart,
And told himself he still had the mountain.
And he made a place there
With my grandmother and his sons and daughters.
But it was not the same.
Like a man who had known a feast
And was placed on rations,
The mountain was enough but not the same.
My Grandfather lived for eighty-nine years.

Many days and many nights he saw;
But I think he may have lived even longer,
If the Wasichu had not stolen part of his heart.

Now the Great Dam of the Kinzu stands,
And the once mighty Allegheny,
Trudges, on its shackled journey,
Like a long puddle drying in the sun.
Ugly stretches of brown-red mud
Smear its long-ago lush banks,
Where the Indian once fished and hunted.
But the smoke from the fire mills,
In the city by the three rivers,
Has been diminished.
"The yellow metal that makes the Wasichu crazy,"[3]
Silenced them.

So, though I want to go away to our Place,
I cannot.
In my heart I can.
But in reality I cannot.
For the Place I love,
Which was a part of me is gone.
But I will remember it.
As long as I live, I will not forget it.

7/22/92

---

[3] From book "Black Elk Speaks" by John Neilhardt.

The Fireplace

Every night, almost, that we spent at the cabin
There was a campfire in the outside fireplace,
And everyone came from the cabin
And went into the cabin as they pleased,
To spend some time around the fire.
We talked of many things
Like sports, politics, the latest news,
What would happen when the dam came through.
Often, we burned a stump.
It sparked and popped all night long
As we sat and talked,
And dreamed and played games.

circa October 1975

The Wedge

Firewood was an ample commodity
At the grandfather's cabin, and a much needed one.
Often, he and his sons would go into the woods
Stump hunting and sawing up trees
Ready to fall or already fallen to the ground.
The great logs would be thrown into the truck,
And taken home where they had to be split.

Too big to be split with an axe,
He used a wedge and a sledge
To split the great logs and stumps.
Often, the young boy would split the logs.
And the old man would stand by smiling
As the youth swung the heavy hammer
Down and down on the square head of the wedge,
His shinny wet sinews rippling in the sun,
As he drove the angled steel home.
The stubborn log would creak and moan,
As the wedge moved closer to its goal,
And then suddenly -
The huge log would give way - splitting apart.
And he would pull up panting,
A young boy, feeling the strength of a man, in a child's heart.

Spring 1973

Time at Our Place

One year we spent our vacation there alone;
Just our family.
It was a good time.
Warm days – cool nights.
The sound of the cricket,
And the tree frog to put us to sleep.
So many things to do.
Badminton with ping-pong paddles,
Hikes in the woods looking for lichens,
Chopping wood,
Walks to the trading post,
Reading books and swimming at the park.

But there was something my father needed to do at home
That made him restless for the city.
So we decided to leave a few days early.
As we drove away from our place
My mother began to cry.
My father offered to go back
But my mother said no.
I don't think she was sad so much about leaving early.
I think she knew what little time was left for our place.

Little time to spend there because of the dam.
She could not bear this thought
And it made her heart heavy.

7/24/92

Foundation Dig

We dug, oh how we dug for the piers,
The auger went deep where the earth
Was soft and free of rock,
When she bottomed out,
Our muscles put steel to stone,
Chipping away, clawing for every inch
To get below the frost line.

When the lumberman came
With his heavy truck,
He eyed the almost vertical road
With a hint of trepidation.
Then he climbed the first hill,
And ran up the second.
After he dropped the load,
The truck slipped sideways,
As it backed out of the narrow slip
Pinning the cab against a young oak.
Our chain saw felled the tree to free the cab.
With chain and boom we pulled and winched her out.
Leaving a muddy muck,
But he was on his way,
And we were relieved.

We kept digging,
Fifteen piers in all,
Until the relentless rain came,
Dropping its water in sheets,
Driving us into cover,
To dry out our wet clothes
And dampened spirits.
We prayed and ate together,
Tired but not beaten,
Ready to build upward tomorrow
For the first time.

July 1, 2011

The Voice of Family

For Uncle Joe

Baseball, a timeless game;
You step on the field and dream of fame.
Pick up your glove, that bat and a ball,
Go down the street to give your friends a call.
You wallop the ball with the strength of youth,
Then round the bases like the storied Ruth.
You take to the field and stop a line drive,
Making the catch with a Brooksian dive.
Then you make a great play on a ball hit late
Making the catch at a galloping gate,
And sizzle a "rope" for an out at the plate.
The game goes on through the height of the day,
Running and throwing play after play.
Then a sinking sun brings you back to time,
And you pack up your gear and cross the lime.

Circa 1981

Inuit

People of the earth,
Nomads in a cold world,
Now man has taken away your tradition
And given you processed food,
And permanent shelter in its place.
You will never again hunt the polar bear and the seal.
No more will you play "cat's cradle"
And tell your children of the raven and the wolf.
No more will you live in houses of ice.
No more will your language tell the ancient stories.

Your children will forget,
And with the forgetting will go
Some special tie with the universe.
With forceful strokes your culture has been washed,
And the mystery and concealment of nature has been quashed.
Innocence has been massacred for the sake of a "better life".

10/11/76

A Man and His House

Spring reveals the weather's harm
To house and hearth from wind and storm.,
The freeze and thaw of hoar and frost.
Tells the toll of winter's cost.

See here this leaky roof and sunken walk.
This softened sash from melting snow
And opened seams in need of caulk.
Doorways buckled and ground made low.

I dress it up with bush and flower.
I cut and mow and add new seed and fertilizer.
I paint, and nail, and brush, and hoe,
All for love I repair and sow.

My house reflects my inner soul.
My need for comfort, direction, purpose and goal.
And with each day that passes by,
We grow in dedication, my house and I.

Circa 1977 – revised 2022

When We Helped

I remember when we used to cut their food
And hold their hand
And take them for walks,
And read them bedtime stories.
We cheered when they ate a lot
And worried when they ate too little.
We answered their questions as best we could
And loved them with a fierce passion.
We taught them the ways of The Christ
And tried to be a living example.
We took them on adventures to the country
And the mountains,
To the cities and the monuments.
We reveled in their victories
And consoled them in defeat.
Memories, all memories,
And our children grown,
To share His light with seed well sown.

June 2001

Noah

When you came to us
"We were like men dreaming."
Elated that time and distance were conquered.
We held you and gazed at you.
When you cooed we laughed,
And talked back at you.
When you laughed we were ecstatic with joy.
What hope you held for us,
And what boundless possibility.
When you left us we were like men without the light,
And we anxiously waited for your return.

June 2004

Longshoreman

He came in the winter months
When the lakes were frozen,
And the ships were safe at port.
When the days grew short,
And the nights grew long,
To pull us on a sled
Across the frozen pond.
Off we'd go,
His skates digging in the ice,
And the winter wind
Cold against our faces.

We went to the cabin
Deep in the woods,
The snow so high on the ground,
And the sun so low in the sky.
We sat by the great wood stove
And ate our kipper snacks and crackers.
We went to the park and watched the jumpers
Fly off the curved snow slopes,
Gliding like birds and landing,
So smoothly, on the snow packed ground.
When we left for home
The flakes were falling fast.

The tire paths were our guide,
And the heater's whrrr our constant companion.

One day in early March
When the winds were strong,
And the days were growing longer,
He came with a kite he had made,
And took me out to fly it.
Higher and higher it climbed
In the patchy blue March sky,
As we watched with the wind against our cheeks,
And the softening ground beneath us.

Then, in early spring,
When winter let go its icy grip,
And the lakers began to move
From their thawing slips,
He was gone again
To ride the Great Lakes,
And move the grain and ore,
To pull hard on the ropes
And set the many knots,
And lock the hatches tight,
To look across the open water
And pass the time in solitude.
Waiting to return again,
In the winter months,
When the sun was low
And the nights were long,
And the ships were safe at port.

July 9, 2005

Life Sketch

There was Little Eddy,
Ray Ray, Kurty Kurt and Ghee.
There was Jonathan John
Dizzy Lizzy, Barberico and Dan
There were thick mangled hands
From digging and plumbing,
Splicing and building
And all that comes between.
And there were tools.
Oh, how there were tools.

There was "All aboard that's going aboard",
And "mandeshevitz",
And "We're headed for the high Sierras".
There was the cabin and the Amish,
And the taste of a homegrown tomato.
There was never a complaint about the food,
As long as it was meat and potatoes.
There was copper and lead and aluminum,
And all the saving of change.
There were the lake boats, flying kites,
Ice skating and riding bikes.

There was compassion and concern,
And "Charity starts in the home".
And chocolate fudge of cheek flushing taste.
All in the mystery of one life lived in love.

July 2005

Not a trace is left
Of where my mother once lived,
The furniture's gone,
The house has been sold.
All that is left are memories to hold.

I'm glad she had time
To spend with us alone.
Doing puzzles and games
And watching her shows.

I hope that God's made her
A place near his throne.
A place she can always
And forever call home.

August 2021

Preparation

On Wednesday Grandma's kitchen was smeared
With dozens of fixings for Thanksgiving Day.
Now dried bread chopped, and tube sausage seared
While grownups dice celery like children at play.

With ritual care the turkey is cleaned.
And women line pie tins with delicate crusts,
Then fill them with lemon, and coconut cream,
And Aunt Jenny's chocolate an absolute must.

Chopped turnip is boiled and acorn squash baked,
While Grandma boils gizzards for gravy to pour.
At the fire, men talk while the logs are raked,
And the coals glow hot to the draft at the door.

Twisted hands sew bird with needle and thread,
And all leave anxious for Thanksgiving bread.

11/28/02

Pitcher

I will go to the mound today,
And bring the heat that makes men pray.
I'll hurl the ball with all my might,
Keeping it low and out of their sight.
Seams will sizzle, and the ball will move,
Staying away from the fatal groove.

I'll throw the curve, then bring it fast,
Striking them out when "the die is cast."
The heat will rise and sweat will flow,
As I mow them down like murderer's row.
Their bats will beat the tepid air.
Jaws will drop, and fans will stare.

They'll say "He's got the stuff today."
And cheers will rise with each new "K".
At the end of the game, at the final out,
Fans will scream and race about.
Yes, I'll play the game the way I love to play.
I'll find myself on the mound today.

11/7/02

When we took him to college,
We said our goodbyes and went home,
Ate dinner, washed the dishes,
And it was late – about nine.
I went to the landing,
Down the three steps,
And locked the door.
Then I knew he wasn't coming home;
Knew he wouldn't need a ride,
Knew there wouldn't be any "catch",
Or a ball game to go to,
Or a conversation at the dinner table.
I was sad for me and happy for him.
I pushed the emotion down under,
And walked up the three stairs
Over to the living room,
To relax, and watch TV with family,
And prepare for another day.

Circa: May 2009

Love's Gift

How do you feel oh little Mary Claire,
In the blanket of love that surrounds you?
Your life fresh and new as the morning dew,
Your hair of Irish red and face so fair,
Nestled in your mother's arms with gentle care.
Human knowledge foretold your chances few,
God's life into your precious soul imbued,
A parent's love your beating heart to share,

Your father there to see you know no harm,
He holds your tiny hands and little feet.
A quilted cover made to keep you warm,
And clothed with love in pink and white replete.
While men like frenzied bees around you swarm,
You grow and move within yourself complete.

October 5, 2005

Just a Thought

I'd like to fly a kite.
One I'd make on my own,
With sticks of delicate balsam wood
And stuff we'd get from home.

We'd cut the sticks just right,
To form a perfect cross;
Lashing the sticks with twine and glue,
So the kite would not get tossed.
And setting the curve in the bow,
We'd knot the tail with strips of cloth,
From sheets as white as snow.
Then with comic papers skintight,
We'd fix the bridle string,
To control its frenzied flight.

And out the door we'd go
With mittens and hat in hand,
And walk to the field at the end of the street
Where the March winds made their stand.
We'd get our bearings straight,
Then set our face to the shivering breeze,
And run, and run as fast as we could
'Til the kite took flight to the wind.

And we'd stand and let it fly,
As high as it could go.
Letting the string pay out its length
As we stood with cheeks aglow.
The kite would sway and bob
As it climbed the rush of air,
Setting itself, of sticks and string,
Against the blue patched snare.

Then satisfied with our skill,
And cold from the March wind's chill,
We'd tow the kite back in again
'Til it hit the soft spring ground.
And thrilled with our success,
Against the gusts we'd press.
Hardly aware of the March wind's roar
As it followed us to our door.
Yes, I'd like to fly a kite.
One I'd make on my own.
With sticks of delicate balsam wood
And stuff we'd get from home.

1/19/02

Leaves fall, wind blows,
Air is bitter.
Water on the windows,
People put a woodhouse
Over their bone house,
The world of reality to leave,
And enter the world of make-believe.

Fall 1973

For R, L, and J ...

"A champion is one who gets up when he can't." Dempsey
I'll never forget the night you asked me for my help
To remake a home that was your dream.
Your wife by your side, brimming with child,
You stood together like twin oaks,
Convicted in your resolve and full of vision.
When you invoked the name of Uncle Dick,
There was little I could say.

So the swing of the hammer and the sledge began,
And the digging and the building followed.
And slowly, with a million motions,
And many hands
The dream and the hope came together,
To make a home for your family which was now three
Made by two, and stronger than ever
In its conviction of love.

9/12/02

Dialogue on a Hero

"Daddy, who was Babe Ruth?"
"He was a baseball player
Who used to eat twenty hotdogs
And twelve bottles of pop.
He loved kids and often
Visited them at orphanages and hospitals.
And he could hit home runs,
Oh, how he could hit home runs.
He was a big man in heart and mind and body.
Do you get the picture?"

Circa 1973

Scary!

I bought a pumpkin for Halloween.
I cut off his top and scraped him clean.
I gave him two eyes and a triangular nose,
Then carved out his teeth in sharp jagged rows.
I gave him a smile that filled me with fright,
Then put in a candle so he'd glow in the night.

Circa October 1988

Forged

I asked my mother once, " Who is my Father?"
She said, "Ahh he was one of the handsome ones,
One of the beautiful ones. But I could not keep him.
He was restless, he was not happy, he thought there was more.
We argued and fought, and he left."

I asked, "Where does he live?"
She told me, but admonished me saying, "Do not go there.
It will only bring you sadness and heartache."

I went, and knocked on his door, and told him who I was.
He denied it, I was not his, he did not want to know me.
He had a life of his own and a family and did not let me in.

I pushed his words down deep into my soul,
And smothered them with layer upon layer of darkness,
So that I could not see them, could not hear their odious sound,
Could not taste their bitterness,
Or feel their harshness,
Could not breath their mephitic odor.

Then, steeling myself, I moved forward, and did not look back,
And forged a life of my own, conceived in caring.
Filling my consciousness and emptiness
With unselfish acts of kindness,

Surrounding myself with those I love.
Strong and unwavering is my commitment,
Tempered in the furnace of experience,
Hoping to hammer out, one small, bright piece,
In the mosaic of human existence.

June 29th 2014

The Voice of Work

Chestnutting

As I take my meal in the breakfast nook,
A chatter and rush goes on in my yard.
The tall chestnut's limbs are all being shook.
In the beauty of fall the squirrels work hard,

Shaking brown nuts from their thorn covered vest,
They run down the trunk to pick-up the treasure,
A mouthful of gold to store in their nest.
The sight of their toil is a welcome pleasure.

Watching the act while the coffee still perked.
A time to reflect on life's simple chores,
Comfort of family and meaning of work,
Glimpsing at nature in gathering stores.

Then with the last bite, a turn at the knob,
I climb in my car, and off to my job.

July '02 to June '03

Steel Life

Coils of steel made from iron and coke,
Hoisted by crane to the rolling mill spot,
Rolled rock hard, then sent off to soak
In furnaces tall with jackets red hot.

We'd finish them off to temper and gauge,
Avoiding the center to roll the sheet flat,
Feeding coil after coil and still the mill raged,
We ordered a "roll change" and took off our hats.

Needing reduction we unleashed the mill.
Steam billowed up as it bit on the steel,
Squeezing its prey like a cat on a kill,
Pulling the strip tight as it tracked on the reel.

Then calling it quits after working all night,
The giant fell silent as we walked out of sight.

June 2003

My Stewardship

I am in a vast sea swimming.
The sea whirls around me.
I swim steadily with direction,
And I become the focal point.
The waves of the sea take direction from me.
They go away from me. They go towards me.
There are other people in the sea.
They swim with a zombie like stroke.
They see me swim my strokes with spirit.
Still, a light lingers in them.
They know. They know.
They hope. They Hope.
From the confusion I leapt into,
I somehow draw meaning around me.
How long before I become tired,
And my stroke takes on a dull, rhythmic routine?

June 10, 1976

Company Man

Working, working day and night,
Pushing out steel silvery bright.
Telling men to do this and do that.
"Band up that steel, put on your hat".
Working past midnight – things quiet and still.
Then arguing, fighting – ready to kill.
Walking on endlessly looking for coils.
When you find them you treat them like a treasure of spoils.
It seems nothing exists except that "damned" plant.
Someday I'm taking vacation; but right now I can't.

Summer 1979

The Banding Line

Steel river of rollers,
Coil after coil coming down
Your endless stream of rapids.
Coils swirl in your whirlpool,
As you band them, girding them tight
For their long journey.

April 1979

Like Monks We Lived

Like monks we lived,
Without the bonds of silence,
Sharing our struggles and our griefs.
No feeble mind could breech us,
No fetid blueblood broke our rule.
Breaking bread for respite,
Waiting, wishing, and hoping for change,
Believing in the resurrection,
And the mystery of the water and the wine.

We thought the white metal
And the red metal would save us.
But it didn't – it couldn't.
While those on the "exchange" made millions,
And those who worked for the state "rode the train,"
We who made something had nothing.

So, we went into the valley each day,
Powerless to change and unable to stop.
Like monks we lived,
Believing in the resurrection,
And the mystery of the water and the wine.

6/19/03

The Anneal

Like Heat Giants the furnaces stood,
Their tall round frames covered with knobs and tubes,
Sat seething in fire quietly contained,
Down deep in the soaking pit.
You could look into their Cyclops eye
And see the red hot hulks of steel coils
Stacked one upon another burning in their bellies,

Having their fill, the bridge crane came,
And lowered its hooked head,
To lift the rotund, hollow trunks off the coil columns.
As the red glow ebbed from their bodies,
The coils looked relieved from their torment.
Then, tall, cool, steel jackets covered them,
And rushing air and water ran through the jackets,
Soothing their baked hides.

Tomorrow they would be skinned on the cold mill,
And sent screaming through the slitter's knives,
Yielding a multitude of offspring coils,
To be shipped, chopped, formed, and drawn
Into a mosaic of jagged pieces,
Creating the modern world of man.

Some pieces would create carnage,
Others would create comfort,
According to the desires, wants, and needs
Deep within, the human heart.

10/20/11

Memories in Steel

I worked in steel for part of my life.
It brought a good living
To my kids and my wife.
The churn of the slitters,
The whirr of the mill,
The smell of the fish oil
Are all with me still.
The bustle of trucks,
And the voices of men,
Got me up in the morning,
And back home again.

I'll never forget the thrill of the call.
To quote on an order for a customer's plant.
To find the right steel and the time to be spent,
And pushing the process to prosper us all.

We had a good group,
We worked day and night.
We were all looking forward,
And the future seemed bright.
But like all things in life,
There had to be change.
And the thrill of the work
Took on the mundane.

Now it's only a memory,
The steel that I sold,
And the warm, hopeful feeling,
Has grown very cold.

But I still hear the cut line pounding away,
And the roll of the pack line,
Sending steel on its way,
To a place near a press
In a customer's plant,
To fill some small need
In the family of man.

June 20th, 2003

The Mill

We cleaned the great green god today.
We picked up gobs of black bile,
That oozed from its steel guts,
We wiped the drool that ran down its face,
From its orange colored engines,
And green tubes leading to its vitals.

We shined it with solvent
Wiping its greasy thick skin clean.
Its air arteries hissed at us as we worked.
Water gushed from its two pipes into a bottomless pit.
We cleaned its knobby head and its inside organs,
So the steel it ate would come out bright.

And it sat there;
Not knowing us or what we did.
Waiting to whirr with rage,
As it gobbled more steel – tomorrow.

May 1979

The Slitter

Coil and recoil, coil and recoil,
The slitter arbor's circular knives turn
As the take-up reel pulls the steel
Through the slitter's sharp teeth.

The re-coiler whirrs as the slitter picks up speed,
The trims of edge scrap rear up like a snake
And the baler laps up the windings
While the narrow bands of steel squeal and screech
Against the take-up separators,
As we watch the reel build up slit coils lap upon lap.

Finally the coil runs out and the tails
Are pulled taught as the operator slows the slitter.
He comes down off his platform
And sets the steel in the jaws of the "mike".

"Wrong gauge" - he calls for the heavy gauge nibblers.
Rata tat tata tat tat the nibbler bites off tiny chips of steel
And cuts the tails cleanly.
At the push of a button the last of the stubborn steel
Leaps out from the arbor
Bucking and lashing at everything in sight.

The re-coiler's arm holds the coils as they're banded
And pushed off the reel to be sent to the
Banding line for eye bands and packaging,
Soon to be punched and drawn and formed
Into the products of a peaceful civilization.

Circa 1979

The Voice of Love

To a Mother from a Father

It was a perfect love.
As perfect as a human love could be.
Through the years we walked life's path,
In two - part harmony.

Arm in arm we danced away
All our pain and sorrow.
Hand in hand we held each day
As precious as the 'morrow.

We blessed our lives in sacrament;
Both ritual and real.
Each moment marked in merriment,
And armed with faith and zeal.
Memories held in timeless time, never to let go.
Thoughts of us, like summertime, melt the winter's snow.

7/18/94

A Pin

A pin can tell you something,
Of what we hold most dear,
Of faith and hope and country,
Of seasons drawing near.

The shapes of shiny silver,
And precious leaves of gold,
Ancient art of crafters,
Beauty bright and bold.

An earthy scene of pine cones,
A flight of gentle doves,
In brilliance and simplicity,
Reflect a person's love.

12/19/09

Being

I'd like to feel you close to me,
And hold you oh so tight.
I'd like to touch your soft, smooth skin,
And kiss your lips goodnight.

The beauty of your threefold being
In body, mind, and soul,
Fills my heart with thoughts of love,
Beyond my own control.

Your ebullience and deep desire,
To let life's river run,
Draws me to your quiet light,
Like flowers to the sun.

My fiery love would soon be quenched,
Like lava to the sea,
If I could find in all the world,
A soul as pure as thee.

12/31/06

If You Were ...

If you were a golden garden flower;
And I was a wandering bumble bee,
I would drink the bloom of your sweet nectar,
And return to the hive in ecstasy.

If you were a beautiful singing bird,
And I became a strong and mighty oak,
I would lend you my limb without a word,
Your melody pouring out as you spoke.

If you were the waves of the ocean blue,
And I was a stone on a sandy beach,
I would long for the waves the shore to reach,
Just to feel the soft, gentle touch of you.

Wishful thoughts to keep within the heart,
As our two souls must never be apart.

7/27/05

I wish I could take your pain
And tuck it deep down into my being,
And suffer it, like a raw wind,
So that you could live and laugh,
And dance and sing your song.
I'd like to take your pain,
And let it seep, deep down into my bones,
And suffer it like a raw wind.

Circa 2018

Moment

Only a moment, in memory, gone,
Since your warm and gentle touch came to me,
And I was caught, like dark before dawn,
Knowing that this sign of love could never be.

Still I stayed, hoping your touch would never end.
Hoping that I could hold your warmth to mine,
Hoping, your soft caress meant more than friend,
Yet knowing my heart could not be with thine.

No words between us passed, nor gaze of eye,
No reciprocated touch for all to know,
No sign of quickened breath or wanton sigh,
Only stillness, knowing the touch would go.

Like bees collecting nectar for their nest,
My soul, in search of love, will never rest.

July 19, 2005

Awe Full Emotion

Love makes one strong
Like the oak tree
That weathers many storms;
Yet soft and compassionate
Like the flower
That radiates much beauty
From the vase it is placed in.

9/8/72

I Saw You

I saw you in the darkness,
I saw you in the night.
I saw you in the evening
When the stars were shining bright.

I saw you in the daylight,
When Apollo rode the sky.
I saw you in the sunset,
So pleasing to the eye.

The gift of you I cherish,
Like gold refined in fire,
Though years leap long between us,
They cannot quench desire.

I pray for grace and strength
To do what's right and true,
And hope you'll always be there
In everything I do.

11/24/10

Love Thoughts

"I have wandered many 'a year
And walked many 'a mile,
But always have I longed for thee,
The star in my bright smile".
****

"With these flowers, I send myself;
With myself, my friendship;
And with my friendship, my love."

****

"My love is so beautiful,
Her heart is warm and tender,
Her touch is soft and caressing.

I am hers – she is mine.
I hope it's like that
For all time."

Circa 1971

The Voice of Time

Autumn

Such great beauty I have seen.
Waves of grain in summer's breeze;
Brilliant color in autumn trees,
From summer's wealth of leaves of green.

Autumn's brilliance brightly shown.
The oak tree's leaves with tint of gold,
And sumac bursting red and bold.
Hints of a God that can be known.

Stalks of corn once lush with kernelled treasure,
Now dried white with amber hue.
Keeping time with nature's cue,
Snow covers earth with blanket white and pure.

In the city, canyons of concrete, block eye and ear,
From nature's wonders once revered.

Circa 1991 Completed 2001

Reflection

When I think of the past,
All those moments,
All those hopes,
I wish I could go back,
And experience them again,
And savor them once more,
With an even greater appreciation.

The splendor of a campus,
The smell of a ball diamond,
The joy, the laughter, the youthful energy.

Some things I wish I had done better.
Some things I wish I had never done.
Some things I just want to experience again
As they were, unchanged.
Some things I wish I had experienced more,
Said more, done more, laughed more,
Knowing that I would not have that moment again.

Our gift of time is so precious.
We don't realize it until it has passed,
And then it is only a memory
To be longed for but never to go back to.

What a gift, the gift of life,
How thankful to be living,
To have those memories is gift itself,
Knowing that the true joy is in remembering,
And going forth to create new memories,
And new rememberings.

Circa 2004

I like to see the honey bees
Reap their specks of gold.
I like to see the bumble bees
Lift their heavy load.

They go from flower to flower,
Stopping for a draught.
Helping every blossom,
Flourish into fruit.

They lead a life of purpose,
Heeding nature's call.
To touch each flower's pubescence,
And pollinate them all.

The cricket does its chirping,
The fire fly lights the way.
The spider weaves its perfect web,
The mantis hunts its prey.

But the bees are always working,
Foraging the fields.
Collecting food to feed their hives,
Increasing nature's yield.

9/26/09

Seasons

In the fall of the year when darkness draws near,
And the leaves on the lawn are a blanket at dawn,
I take up my rake and I sweep, and I sweep,
Gathering leaves into bright colored heaps.
Then stuffing them into large plastic bags,
To put by the road with the garbage and rags.
The wind at my breath puffs crisp and clear,
And the cold autumn air is red at my ear.
Tables and chairs move with scampering feet,
The final reminder of summer's slow heat.
When all is away and the yard is laid bare,
I think of the snow and the short winter days,
Of the warmth of a fire and flakes in the air,
The comfort of home in the dark of the year,
And the hope of a spring, which is ever so near.

November 5, 2003

Summer Nights

We used to sit out on warm nights like this
On the porch next door in the warm balmy breeze
Neighbors would stop on the sidewalk to chat,
To talk about the weather and things like that.
Children would play and hide behind trees
With the sun gone down in the darkness of night
Warm hearts of friendship provided the light
A time when people felt closer than now
And men earned their living by the sweat of their brow.
And porches were places where we ended the day.

Circa 1995

Spring Awakening

Spring's first warm days bring people
Peeking outside their doors to see if it is really true,
Then confident of their meteorological calculation,
(a hand stretched out the door),
They venture outside and they see signs.

The dirt and debris winter's white coat hid so well,
The wet soggy ground that squishes like jell.
The first green shoots of early spring flowers,
The crocus, the hyacinths, and daffodils,
And the soft cotton buds of the pussy willow.

Signs of new life appearing and growing each day,
Pushing their way through the soft wet clay,
Children on tricycles with sneakers on feet,
And the attraction of puddles to new sneakers so neat.
Fathers and mothers taking up brooms,
Sweeping and cleaning garages and rooms.
Seeing neighbors after winter's long separation,
Catching up on the news, sharing spring's expectations.

It seems all worthwhile to go through winter's strife,
And see the promise of spring and the hope of new life.

Circa 1980 – Revised May-June 2003

Time Travel

Fifty miles off the Yucatan, in the blue Caribbean,
Travelling east for Jamaica,
They ran headlong into the vaunted trade winds.
The welcome winds of fortune
For swift schooners of an age forever gone.

The twenty-eight thousand ton leviathan
Facing gale force winds,
Galloping through the ten foot swells,
Spewing spray seventy feet high
Into the beating heat of the sun.

At night the people gathered,
To hear Schubert, Bach and Beethoven
On the weeping violin,
And forget for a moment
Their fierce fight against the surging sea.

Just as fiddlers of old
Entertained weary sailors,
On dark dimly lit nights
In the cramped quarters
Of the cargo cutters.

For twenty-two hours
Wind and sea battered the bulkhead bow,
Lashed and slashed at the huge steel carcass,
And still they plied the perilous passage.
At dawn they moored in Jamaica.

And impoverished people there,
Welcomed the green paper
Of ship bound landlubbers,
Eager for gifts, goods, and adventure
On the hardbound land.

October 2005

Bright the Dawn

Bright the dawn,
Beautiful the day,
In early spring
When robins play.
In the clearing, a gentle fawn,
Fruit of winter's hardships borne.
To rocks and trees the insects cling,
Awaiting warmth the sun will bring.
From garden homes the tulips rise,
And shed the shroud of earth's disguise.
Among the cities and the fields,
Hands toil now with strength and zeal.
From peak and valley nature shows its scene,
Painting pictures of newborn spring.

April 26. 1991

I see your gait is better now,
You're getting back your sway.
Your laughter fills the room again,
Your smile lights up the day.
The gift of life's a mystery.
In its seasons, time and place.
With grace and perseverance,
You'll soon be back on pace.

11/22/11

First Snow

It brings warmth and a sense of hope.
It is a white blanket of security.
The moon shines its soft light upon it
Creating a peaceful feeling.
The sun shines its bright light upon it
Giving it a brilliance one can hardly look at.
Through the front windows of a warm house,
The street light shines upon the snow
Making the flakes twinkle and sparkle.
Frost on the windows gives the streetlight a radiant glow.
"All is calm, all is bright."
For on a cold winter's night a child was born
Who filled the world with hope.
New fallen snow gives you that feeling.
Coming out of work at night
The snow-covered land has a visibleness.
The darkness is not so dark.
Like the newborn Christ Child
It illuminates a darkened world.
And brings a certain stillness in the air,
As if time had stopped.
As if nature's work had become a work of art.

Circa: December 1975

For You – Remembrance ("Tammy's Story")

I went back to my old neighborhood today.
It really hadn't changed much,
A few more run - down homes.
Ted's Used Cars was still in business,
My boyfriend bought his first car there.
The corner delicatessen was all boarded up,
My girlfriend Sherie and I used to go to that store
With our nickels and dimes.
We used to buy candy and pop
And sit on the front steps of the deli,
Enjoying our sugary treasure.

Sherie lived just down the street from the store,
Until her mother was accosted,
Then she moved away, far into the country.
(We didn't know why she moved,
Until we were older,
And then we understood.)
I still would go and see her.
We would play all day outdoors in the fresh air,
And indoors, when the weather was dreary, around the Cannabis
Pretending we were in the jungle.
Sherie's mom was a sort of an artist,
She did her own decorating

And it was very original and tasteful,
She did her best to make a home for her daughter.

Sometimes I'd go to my Gramma's,
She was a broken vessel of human love.
I walked through the narrow aisles in her house,
On either side of the paths there were
Stacks of papers and all sorts of stuff.
She was so full of love and warmth,
I never thought her collecting habits were unusual.
There was always an abundance
Of dolls and toys to play with,
And it was so peaceful there.

Some years later Gramma's health failed.
We tried desperately to care for her at home.
I was older then and trying to set my course in life,
And my mother would ask me to come home
And watch Gramma.
It was hard – real hard,
Gramma's body and mind were failing.
Dementia and incontinence,
The enemies of old age,
Tormented and taunted her, and tested us,
As we struggled to relieve her suffering.
Eventually we couldn't care for her anymore.
We sent her to a nursing home.
She didn't live long once she left our house.
We laid her to rest quietly.
She was at peace,
I'll never forget her.

We still see each other - Sherie and I.
But those days of youthful innocence,
They were the best.
When we were together the world

Seemed like a wonderful place,
Full of adventure and endless possibility.
I'd like to see the world once again,
Through the eyes of a child.

Perhaps someday far off in the future,
My kids, (I'm raising citizens of the world you know.)
Will find someone nice and raise families.
Then I'll see the world through the eyes
Of those precious children.
I'll watch them grow, and experience each day,
In their innocence and awe.
I'll listen to their quips and laugh at their antics
No one speaks the truth truer than a child.
And we'll be one big extended family,
Strong as an oak with its straight, tall trunk
And its sturdy limbs,
Breaking bread together,
And living in a community fashioned out of love.

11/24/13

The Voice of Faith

Advent Log

An Advent log to mark the time,
When Christ would come to save mankind.
We light the candles one by one,
As we wait for God's own Son.

All praise to you Oh God the Christ,
For your great act of sacrifice,
To come to earth as God made flesh,
So humbled in your wooden crèche.

Prayer and song we give to You,
To grant us strength, our hearts renew.
You came to us as tiny child,
To show us power's love so mild.

Prepare the way for this good gift,
With rough hewn log, the cross to lift.
An Advent log to mark the time,
When Christ would come to save mankind.

December 3, 2005

Ave Maria

A beautiful woman sang last night,
To the Virgin Mother and the Child of Light.
Hands all gnarled and body bent,
She sang of love from heaven sent.
Her voice so weak,
Her heart so strong,
Her notes plucked heartstrings,
Tears ran down.
And when she stopped, all kept silence there,
In reverence for the gift so fair.
How great God's love for man so small,
How great man's love for God of all.

April 1988

Winter's Reflection

When the sun in the sky is setting low,
And the ploughman's land is frozen sod,
The earth receives her blanket of snow,
And there seems a deeper presence of God.

Evergreens in thick white frost,
Remind us of the Virgin Birth.
Precious ransom for our cost,
Giving each a special worth.

Ox and lamb with clouds of breath,
Gather 'round the God made flesh.
That night, the hope of conquered death
Springs forth, the human heart refreshed.

All around we look for love,
And fail to seek it from above.

11/7/91

A Gift to Cover Us

I fashioned a table of wood
To give to a loved one,
A parent, a sibling, a grandchild, a friend,
I went to the forest to find the finest wood.
I took it home and debarked it,
Then sawed it into thin slabs.
I glued and doweled the flat pieces
And rounded the legs on a lathe.
Then I sanded and sanded,
To the finest finish ever created.
I found the perfect stain,
And sealed the table with urethane
To protect its precious beauty,
Then gave it to my loved one
To complete his abode
And to cherish and hold dear.

I returned sometime later,
And saw the remains of my masterpiece.
It was drilled and pierced,
And painted in dark colors with grotesque images
One would see in nightmares.

I was deeply saddened.
I believed in my loved one,

Believed they would value
What was so freely and lovingly given to them.
They defaced my work,
And defaced me, as they were made in my image.

How beautiful is the gift of the skin,
The largest organ of the body,
In all its simplicity and complexity,
And all its many stages.
The skin of a young baby so fresh and new,
The skin of a man at work glistening with sweat,
The skin of a young woman so soft and smooth,
The skin of a teenager bursting with life,
The skin of the aged wrinkled and worn.
Our skin comes in colors of white, red, brown and black.
It protects us from infection,
And heals us when we are wounded.

It opens its pores to cool us in the heat of the day,
And closes itself to keep us warm.
It tells us of danger from heat and from harm,
It shows our emotions in goose bumps and blush.

Man with his puny ego thinks he can do better,
But he can't, he only hurts and insults his Creator.
The skin, a thing of precious beauty, a gift entrusted to us.

5/12/12

Mercy

"yet unwilling to expose her to shame, he decided to divorce her quietly" (Mt 1:19) NASB

When I thought of her, I felt her misery – **misericordia**,
In my heart, and I knew her fear.
But when I saw her I felt hope,
When I held her I felt innocence,
When I heard her voice, I felt faith.

And I was prompted to remain with her by a mighty power.
And I showed my love for her all my life,
In the going and the coming,
In the working and the playing,
In the worry and the hope,
For her and for her Son,
Who became the joy and purpose of my life.

12/7/02

Mother Theresa

She is as a god the Hindus say.
Serving the poor day by day.
Patiently she gives them care.
Easing the burden of the cross they bear.
To the dying alone she gives dignity,
Uplifting their souls for eternity.
Mother and child seek her touch,
To feel the love they miss so much.
And the world looks on with anger and delight,
Not daring to harm God's awful might.
For God saw fit to show His power
In the faith and strength of a little flower.

Circa - February 1991

Loss

In the still of the night she slipped away,
Forever to be with her Lord the Groom.
No more to spend with us a summer's day,
Or see the beauty of a flower's bloom.

For she is with the Father and the Son,
And reached the perfect realm of fullest bliss.
The body of her work forever done,
And always close to Christ her heart in His.

Though we on earth are saddened at her loss,
And miss her boundless love and energy,
Our God and Brother was ransomed for her cost,
And we have left the gift of memory.

Although her great soul must from us depart,
Her acts of love live on within each heart

August 11, 2005

Evergreen

Evergreen, everlasting
Unchanging sign of hope,
Your presence is ever felt
As you stand in my home
Decorated with man's creations
As if your natural beauty was not enough.
How great and humble you are.
You do not speak nor read nor write,
Yet, the warmth you bring
And the effect you have, uplifts man's spirit.
You are the symbol of our hope of what we might be
Someday in our union with the Trinity.
We know this is possible through the Godman
Whom you so perfectly symbolize.

1/13/75

Easter Greeting

That first Easter the Father
Gave the Son a special grace.
In a flash of power and light
The great stone grave was opened,
And behold, the Christ came forth
To save the human race.

May his perfect love embrace us,
And set our spirits free,
And the hope and joy of Easter
Be ours eternally.

4/5/90

Praise You

Praise You, Lord God of all creation,
All creation praises you and it is good.
For you have done marvelous things among your people,
There is so much to thank you for Lord,
For the beauty of a spring day,
For the birth of a newborn baby,
For the abundant food that grows from the earth,
For a man and a woman deeply in love,
For the raging seas,
And the heavens that crack thunder for Your glory,
For life itself in all its fullness.
I praise You Lord and am held in awe.
When I look up at the heavens,
And see the vastness of the universe,
I see how tiny and small man is,
I am humbled and deeply moved to know
That despite my insignificance – I am loved.

The Voice of
Desert Places

Darkness

I'd like to live in the big city alone,
And walk down shadowed streets of silent stone.
While some people smile and greet,
Most pass, like zombies
To destinations unknown.

Neon lights fill the air,
As ladies of the night come out,
Eyes and teeth burning bright,
To bring a one-night lover to their lair.

Night goes on and slowly swallows up
All noise, all light, and sleep prevails.

August 1976

Sorrow

Grieving, grieving, filled with grief,
Heads bowed low in disbelief.
Death comes swift like blazing light,
Then comes the agony of deep dark night.

Circa 1980

Lament

Gone the family people,
Selfish people take their place.
They all come from the human race,
But something has changed them.

The local bank has replaced the steeple,
Family bible cast aside for gleaming gem,
Self - centered substitutes for self-sacrifice.

"Turn back o man", from your selfish ways,
Live a life that in spirit pays.
We cannot control our destiny,
But only guide it a little.

Take heed, take heart its time for change,
To change our aim for a "further range."

Circa 1975

After 911

At Mass, they didn't sing God Bless America,
And a young man rushed out early with his son.
"I read it already", he snapped as he was offered the bulletin.
He hurried to his gargantuan SUV and drove away
To gorge his senses with some grotesque experience.
And thousands of miles away a man worried
About how he would feed his family
And where he would find shelter for them,
While in the sanctuary the Priest waited reverently
For the second stanza of the recessional hymn
And then proceeded to the open door.
And the young man kept running.

11/18/01

A Nephew's Prayer

How does one describe a life of Christian service
Rooted in love?
A great philosopher once stated,
"What can be shown cannot be said."
There are not enough words in the universe,
To describe the countless acts of charity
My remarkable Aunt performed.
They can only be witnessed.
They can only be felt.
They can only be remembered.
John wrote in his First Epistle,
"Beloved, let us love one another for love is from God."
That was her creed,
Endless love,
Unconditional love,
Understanding love,
And with this love came courage,
Courage to face many trials,
Courage to endure many heartaches,
Courage to witness, to the Gospel, of Jesus Christ.
I am blessed to have known her,
To have walked with her,
And shared with her,

And now, I must remember her,
And live by her example of courage and love.

John F. Carver
1/24/05

The sun was setting
As we walked up to Main Street
The buildings blocked the horizon,
And all that could be seen were the bright rays
Of the sun piercing upward through the clouds.
It was a radiant scene that said,
"How beautiful are the sights of the earth,
How sheltered and secure they make man feel."
By day the sun shines through the atmosphere,
To create a blue canopy for our heads.
At night the sun's absence makes the sky turn black,
And a million specs of light shine bright
Revealing the stars a trillion miles away.
The creator gives us sight to see,
But not to comprehend the vastness of the universe.

May 1978

We had a secret garden.
We watered it each day.
We used to laugh and carry on,
And watch the children play.

The garden had such color.
Of red and green and gold.
Reflections of our inner being,
A beauty to behold.

But then the garden faltered.
Its days were filled with drought.
The water that its flowers craved
Was dammed with fault and doubt.

The shriveled blooms of summer,
In temporary pain,
Hope their fate will someday end
With gentle drops of rain.

9/26/09

The Voice of Meditation

"The Kingdom of God is not a matter of eating and drinking but of justice and peace and ... joy of the Holy Spirit" Romans 14:17 NIV

How true Lord,
So many of us horde You.
We look to You for consolation and comfort.
We go to Mass and eat Your body and drink your blood.
Then we go home and somehow leave You behind.
Where is the joy I should be showing the world Lord?
This is a serious business being a Christian.
Yet it is a joyful task because it is Your business.

Circa 1978

Sin

Sin is the loss of innocence. It is the forfeit of trust for our own selfish curiosity. How many times have I forgotten God, thinking I could take care of myself. Sin is not so much a failure to obey as it is a failure to love. And with love comes trust, and with trust comes faith, and with faith comes hope, and with hope comes possibility and room for growth outward and upward.

Sin is lack of communication. It is inwardness, Lord, so often I have stopped talking, so often I have thought of myself. It is hard Lord in an imperfect world. But the world is imperfect because we are imperfect. Man is the keeper of the world. You gave him dominion over the earth. If a farmer does not take care of his fields they grow scraggly and bear no fruit. We have let the world grow hostile and wild because of our imperfection and our failure to work with you and to surrender ourselves to you. It is only when we die to self and put our hope and trust in You that we conquer sin and attain true and everlasting happiness in the infinite and ever faithful light of your presence. Help me Lord to turn away from sin and to find perfection in You.

Circa 1978

Meditation John 15:9-17 NABRE

Lord you talked about love,
You presented a sequence,
A circle of love.
"As the father loves me, so I love you.
Love one another,
Greater love has no man than to give up his life for a friend."
And if one of these links is broken there is no love.
If the Father stops loving the Son,
If the Son stops loving us,
If we stop loving each other,
Then the circle of love breaks,
And the progress toward the Kingdom is impeded.
Love is a boundless thing.
Love overcomes human limit I was once told,
And it's true.
We are beings who are limited
Biologically, socially, spiritually, nationally,
But love overcomes these limits,
Not so much by eliminating them,
But rather by helping us to accept these limits,
And live with them.
And in this living in love,

Somehow a change, a transformation is brought about
In ourselves, and maybe even the world.

We talk about giving up one's life for a friend.
Many of us will never give up our physical lives,
But each us die a little every day,
How often we make sacrifices for our families,
Our children or our spouses.
All this to keep the circle of love going,
And complete, in some small way, the Kingdom of God.

6/17/77

Martha and Mary

Lord you've been on the road for a long time. You recently commissioned your disciples to go out and preach to the towns and villages healing and casting out devils in your Name.

Things have not been going well. And You come to the village of Martha and Mary needing rest and needing comfort. Mary sits by Your side and listens to your problems. She smiles and laughs at the frustrating jokes you make about your problems. And she is saddened when you talk seriously and deeply about your inmost feelings, fears, and convictions.

Meanwhile, Martha busies herself with preparing food and a table. But you do not need food for the body at this time, so you rebuke her when she tries to call Mary from your side. Lord, it is good to know that You know what it's like to have a good listener and comforter around. Because now when I come to You I am not afraid that You will not understand. You know me. You know what it is to be comforted and listened to. Help me Lord to be like Mary - not to be so anxious to fulfill others needs with all kinds of rushing around and serving; jumping to help people, but really leaving the person alone in trying to help. Thanks to Your Father that Mary was there for You, or You would indeed have felt very lonely and empty with Martha in the kitchen, serving you something you did not need.

Circa 1977

Genesis 3:14-15 NIV

A vague promise Lord,
We are so much like You.
A child does something wrong.
A mother scolds and punishes him.
Later, feeling sorry for the child and loving him so,
She comforts him and consoles him,
And makes a vague promise.

The next day, the next week, the next month,
She fulfills that promise Lord.
It may be a small toy,
Or a pair of mittens,
Or a trip to the candy store;
But the gift is given.
The vague promise becomes reality,
And is fulfilled.

You knew us Lord.
You knew us so completely,
And loved us so much,
That you gave us the ultimate gift – Your Son
And He was devoured and consumed by this world,
But Your Son rose up from this temporal flesh,
And conquered sin and death,

And took on new life.
And this new life lives in the world
Through His power and glory.

Circa 1977

The Deceit of Science

A Reflection on the Three Mile Island crises – April 1,1979

What has science done for us? Has it really unlocked the secrets of the universe? Has it explained away our, "foolish religious superstitions" and made our lives more wholesome and comfortable?

No it has not. Science is the ultimate step, the culmination, the epitomy of man's presumptuous attitude toward God and His Universe.

Look at the catastrophe of Harrisburg's Three Mile Island nuclear power plant. Man studied the atom, and learned how to split it. He learned how to release enormous amounts of energy with it. And what did he do with this knowledge? First he used it to create a devastating, hideous atomic bomb. Then he created nuclear power plants like the one in Harrisburg, Pennsylvania. And these plants have become America's bane. They stand poised, their chains drawn taught, ready to strike, spewing their lethal doses of radiation, and raining it down upon man, plant, and beast at the slightest malfunction, the slightest slip of man's hand. And they say science gives us control, and provides us with un-thought of treasures. Better those treasures remain buried.

Science has provided us with the means of communication. We can talk and communicate with one another, exchanging ideas and gaining greater knowledge of what is going on in the world at each moment. Yet with all these means of communication, science has failed to enable men to communicate what is in their hearts. It fails to show us how to understand and accept each other's beliefs, convictions, and attitudes. With all this communication science has provided, man still cannot live in harmony with his fellow man.

Science has given us the gift of transportation - incredible mobility. We can move huge cargoes of goods halfway around the world. Yet in many countries children suffer from malnutrition and even starve to death while in other countries farmers are paid for not planting because there is no market for the food.

Science has given us the gift of synthetic products made from numerous combinations of chemicals. Yet the wastes from these chemicals have contaminated the workers. The wastes have seeped into our food and water supply. The wastes have poisoned our children. Like King Midas our "touch" has become deadly to the very things we love.

And in all that science has given, man has found nothing but misery, and suffering, and doubt, and greater imbalances among the countries of the world than existed before science bestowed its gracious gifts upon us.

Science cannot change the hearts of men. Only God can do that. God's Son came on this earth 2000 years ago to teach us how to live. We still have not learned. Yet we picked up the teachings of science rather quickly. When will men learn the lessons that are truly worthwhile and stop reveling in the nonsense of this transient, temporal, physical life? When will men embrace the Resurrection and turn to the power of Jesus' love? How long? Not long. For in God's mind a month is but a second and a year but an hour.

The Vine and the Branches

The Priest talked about the vine and the branches passage. He talked of trimming your branches. He mentioned how everyone was interested in diets. He pointed out that we must do this in a spiritual sense. Sometimes God Himself does the trimming. We are trimmed by him through our sufferings, our anxieties, our trials. In more concrete terms this can be expressed as a death in the family, failure of one's health, lay-off from work, problems with the children, or any number of other things.

But there are ways of keeping our own selves trimmed too. We do this through our prayer life, the practice of patience with our children and those around us, the control of our anger, fasting, generosity to those in need, spiritual reading, and a host of other things.

Our society has let its branches grow without trimming. Individuals have not pruned themselves. We have all become great tangled bushes. This happens when we as individuals gratify the self. The more we gratify the self, the larger the self becomes. Soon we begin to violate the rights of others in the attempt to gratify the self. When others do the same the whole political, economic, social, and religious community becomes a tangle of dissent and disregard. Our bushes shade out the sun and so we only appear fruitful at the top or surface of ourselves. We must not grow like weeds, but straight and tall like mighty oak trees.

5/22/76

Ash Wednesday

Ashes – sign of destruction,
Of tearing down – black, dark.
But from these ashes
We are raised like the Phoenix,
To a new life in Christ.

By divorcing ourselves from an imperfect world,
Dying to self, symbolized in these ashes,
We are born again through Christ.
He is both destroyer and builder.
He makes destroying possible,
Because he is our help in rebuilding.

For in all destruction there is rebuilding.
Land is flooded
And the farmer plants again next season.
Houses burn and are rebuilt.
Wars are waged,
And from the ashes a new society rises.
The earth is forever consuming itself,
And making new again.

So the young Priest says,
"Repent and receive the Good News".

Ash Wednesday, a reminder
That we must die, to have new life.

Circa February 1975

Short Stories

Kite Flying

One March day my Uncle Eddy, my mother's brother, came over to the house. He was a young man of about 23, about 6 feet tall, with strong rounded shoulders and imposing size. I liked to see him because he always had something interesting and adventurous to do.

And sure enough he had something new in store for me that day. He had brought a kite with him. It was a colorful one made from the funny pages of the Sunday Comics. There were cross-sticks of delicate balsam wood and a long white tale made from strips of knotted bed sheets. It looked like he had enough kite string to fly it up past the clouds.

Eagerly, I grabbed my winter coat and cap, which my mother buttoned and fastened. Then on with my boots and out the door I went. We rode over to a nearby park, got the kite out of the car, and walked to the middle of the field. My uncle looked for the direction of the wind as the kite wiggled and twisted in his hand, its thin paper skin crackling and rippling, eager for flight. Then, finding the direction, he held the kite up and ran into the wind holding the string way up over his head and pulling the string and letting it out. I ran with him as fast as I could. As he ran I heard the sound of his big round toed work boots squishing in the soft spring earth. But the kite kept coming down.

Each time it fell he patiently rolled the kite string up and adjusted the bridle, deepened the bow and took off or added more tail. Too tired I stood by the side of the field and watched. Once again, he let the kite out into the wind. This time it took off higher and higher with each pull of the string. The wind was gusting strong and lifting the kite as if it wanted to take it from us. My uncle stopped running and left the work to the wind. The kite rose still higher zigzagging toward the clouds.

My uncle let me hold the spindle for awhile and I could feel the pull and yearn for string as if it were trying to reach for something. Finally, there was no more string left and my uncle took the spindle and held it as we watched the kite floating and swinging in the cloudy blue sky anxiously pulling and trying to free itself.

After some time we slowly began pulling the kite back in. It was like a little tug of war between the kite and us. Finally, the kite began to spin and dive and fell to the ground. When we reached the kite, we looked it over. Our kite had taken the pummeling of the March winds well.

We walked hurriedly back to the car, our faces flushed from the March winds and our fingers a little numb. The purring warmth of the car's heater felt good and made me sort of sleepy. "Well, did you enjoy flying a kite?" my uncle asked. "Yes," I said, "can we do it again someday?" "Sure," my uncle replied, "maybe next time we'll have a little more luck and the wind won't be so chilly." That was the last thing I remember until my uncle stirred me to wake up when we reached home.

Circa 1978

The Big Sleep

With the first rays of sunshine that came into his bedroom, Kevin jumped out of bed. The wiry, blonde, blue eyed six-year -old hurriedly dressed. He put his socks on first to insulate his feet from the cold hardwood floor. Then on went his corduroys; a shirt and sweater, a pair of shoes and off he went downstairs.

He quickly ate hot oatmeal with honey and milk his mother had made for him. He was anxious to get outside, for something seemed different to him as he looked out the kitchen window. He scurried down from his seat, got his jacket and hat from the hook in the hall and was out the door.

Something had changed, he was sure of it now. The leaves of the trees had changed. Yellows, golds and reds filled the trees with bright color. Last night's blustery winds put a light coat of leaves across the front lawns. "A leaf fort!" Kevin thought. He ran back to the garage to get a rake. As he turned the corner of the house he heard shaking and rattling. He looked up and saw the great Chestnut tree, its branches drooping with the fall harvest. Squirrels were scurrying about shaking the branches of the trees and chestnuts were plopping on the ground below. The ground beneath the tree was covered with the large, shiny brown nuts and one of the squirrels ran down the trunk, stuffed two nuts in his mouth, and ran back up again in a terrible hurry. They had built a huge nest way up in the tree and were storing the nuts there.

Kevin could not believe his eyes. He took his hat off and went over to fill it with the autumn treasure. He left some for the squirrels though, because he knew they needed them for the long winter and besides, they had done most of the work.

He ran back to the garage to get the leaf rake and as he ran back out the driveway he noticed many of the flowers were dead and drooping. The wicked frost had killed them. Kevin felt sad for a moment but the leaf fort came back to mind and he was off. His friend David was out now and together they raked a huge pile of leaves. They built the walls of their fort waste high and played "Cowboys and Indians". They still had a large pile of leaves left and they ran and jumped and dove in them. Overhead a flock of geese honked their way south.

As they were playing, the door of the house swung open and Kevin's mother called him for lunch. Walking to the house he noticed people out washing storm windows with vinegar and hot water and putting them up to get ready for the winter. Taking the rake back to the garage he noticed a lone bumblebee darting in and out among the drooping Snapdragons. The bee could open their little mouths and stick his whole body way down in the flower looking for the last drop of nectar for the long winter. Kevin thought of his grandfather the beekeeper. His grandfather told him the bees were making their last forage of Buckwheat and Goldenrod and this was the best and richest of honeys. "Their hives must be sticky with the stuff," Kevin thought.

When he got into the house his mother had a toasted cheese sandwich ready for him with a tall glass of milk and cookies for dessert. While he was eating Kevin said, "Mom I don't know if I like autumn or not. I mean, the leaf forts are great, and the pumpkins are fun to carve, but everything seems to be dying, everything seems to be getting ready to go to sleep." "Well dear", his mother replied, "things are dying and going to sleep, but in some ways autumn is the richest time of the year because of its brilliant colors and all the fruits and vegetables that grandma and I are able to can and store for the winter." "See", he said, "even you're putting stuff away for the big sleep." His mother laughed and said, "Come now, it's time for a nap." Kevin was tired too. The fresh, crisp autumn air had made him tired. His mother tucked him in and gave him a kiss. Soon he was asleep dreaming of bees and honey, leaf forts and chestnuts, storm windows and pumpkins; all the richness that autumn brings.

Circa 1977

Strength

One day God the Father, Jesus His Son, and the Holy Spirit were sitting together in perfect union. Jesus was eager to tell his Father something.

"Dad, guess what, I'm the strongest person in heaven. I wrestled St Michael, all the Cherubs and Seraphs, Gabriel and Arial and beat them all.

"The only one stronger than me is you Dad and I know I couldn't wrestle you."

"That's very good Son," said God the Father. "But remember, with strength comes responsibility. I have a mission I've been working on for about 4000 years. I need someone to go down to earth and teach the humans how to live. They're an irascible bunch – always fighting and arguing and hoarding wealth. They tried to become like Me and lost their spot in heaven. Since you are the strongest, won't you go down to earth and teach them the way to live so they can have eternal salvation?

"You'll have to become a human being, experience all the joys and struggles of life in time, and suffer and die on a cross. The humans will call it the tree of salvation. They'll even bring a tree into their house on your birthday each year to remind them of everlasting life and the cross which was their salvation."

"Dad, I'd like to," Jesus said "but how am I going to do it?

"There's a young woman called Mary who lives in Nazareth," God said. She is the only woman free of sin. She will bear you as a child and be your mother – mothers were one of the best ideas I created. There's a man named Joseph who will watch over you as a father and you will grow into a young man and preach among the people. I'll be with You through your suffering and death and raise you up on the third day so you can come back to me and bring the humans with you. It will take great humility to do this Son. Will you do it for Me?"

Jesus thought for a moment. What would the angels think of him in such a humble estate? Would they snicker and laugh at him behind his back? Would the strongest be looked upon as weak? He knew it had to be done and because he was in Union with his Father he knew that he, Jesus, was the only one to do it, as he was the strongest in heaven after His Father.

"I'll do it Dad!" he said.

And so, you know the rest - our salvation history. Christ came into time with Mary's yes and Joseph listened to the angel and took Mary as his wife. The angels exalted His birth and never wavered from His side There was great joy, hard work and suffering. And Christ Jesus did it all because he was the strongest. He trusted His Father and gave us the way to eternal life.

And instead of saying "The End", let us all say THE BEGINNING!

Remember: with strength comes responsibility

December 24th 2019

Printed in the United States
by Baker & Taylor Publisher Services